THOMAS
& FRIENDS™

HOW TO USE AR

1  Download the free iOS App from Apple App Store or the Android App from Google Play. Launch the ThomasAR app to open the home page. Tap the play button (▶) to start your Thomas Augmented Reality experience.

Get ready to see Thomas in your room!

2  Four of the pages in this book have red Augmented Reality boxes on them. When you get to one of these pages, place the open book on the floor or a chair, making sure the pages are flat. Hold your mobile device up to the open pages and stand back so you can see the whole book on your screen.

3 Then watch Thomas and his friends come to life with Augmented Reality!

What you need - system requirements
This product works with the following Apple and Android devices: Apple — devices using iOS version 4.3 and above, including iPhone 3GS and upwards, iPod Touch 4G and upwards, and iPad 2 and upwards. Android — devices using Android version 4.0 and above, such as the Samsung Galaxy Nexus and the Asus Google Nexus 7 tablet.

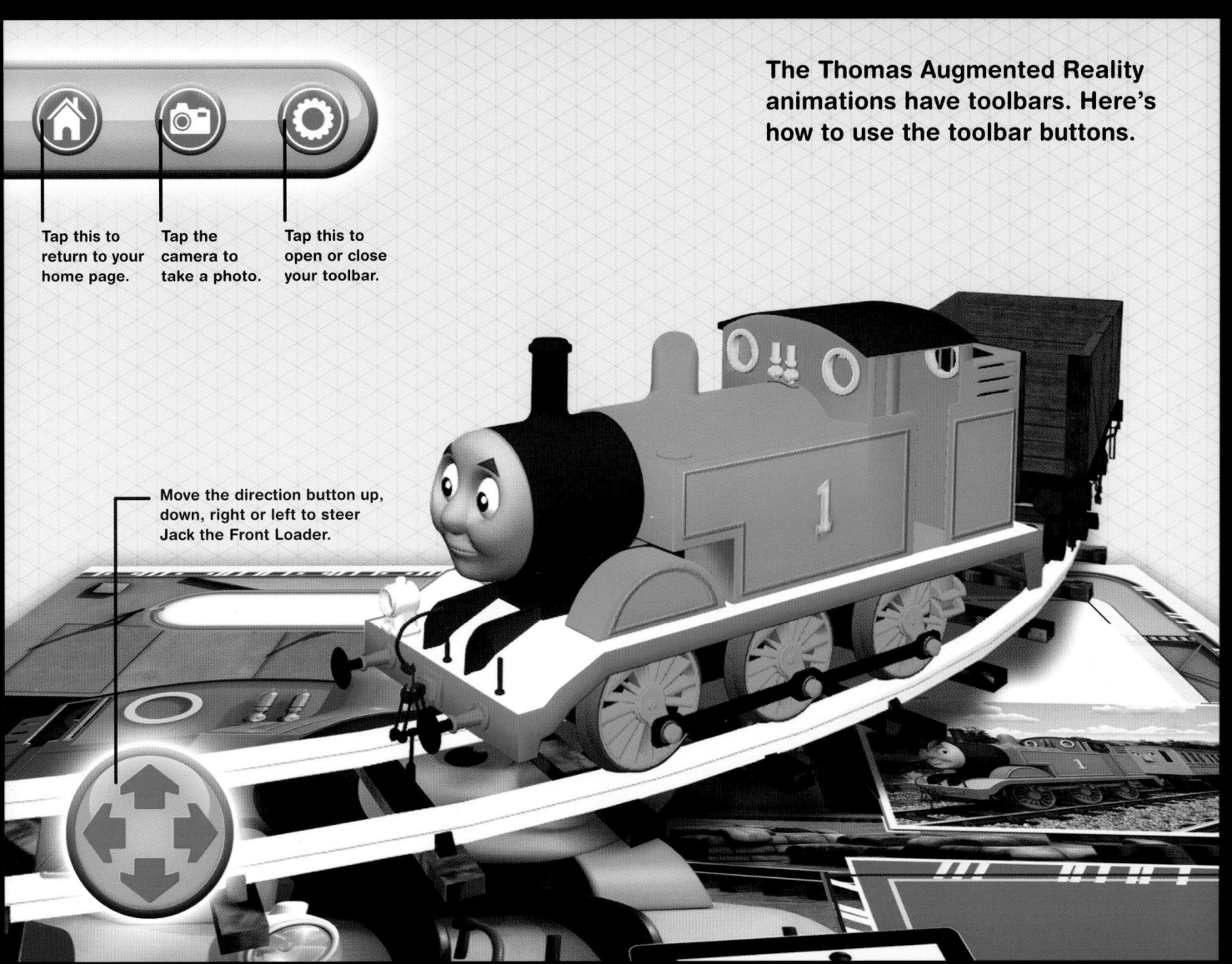

The Thomas Augmented Reality animations have toolbars. Here's how to use the toolbar buttons.

Tap this to return to your home page.

Tap the camera to take a photo.

Tap this to open or close your toolbar.

Move the direction button up, down, right or left to steer Jack the Front Loader.

Need some help?
If you've got a problem, check out our website:
www.carltonbooks.co.uk/icarltonbooks/thomas

THIS IS A CARLTON BOOK

Text and design:
© Carlton Books Limited 2013.

Published in 2013 by Carlton Books Limited,
An imprint of the Carlton Publishing Group,
20 Mortimer Street, London, W1T 3JW.

A catalogue record for this book is available
from the British Library.

ISBN: 978-1-78312-011-6
Printed in Dongguan, China.

With special thanks to Mason Parsler
Writer: Emily Stead

HiT entertainment

Thomas the Tank Engine & Friends

CREATED BY BRITT ALLCROFT

Based on the Railway Series by the Reverend W Audry
© 2013 Gullane (Thomas) LLC. A HIT Entertainment company.
Thomas the Tank Engine & Friends and Thomas & Friends
are trademarks of Gullane (Thomas) Limited.
Thomas the Tank Engine & Friends and Design is Reg. U.S.
Pat. & Tm. Off.

CARLTON KiDS

Welcome to SODOR

A long time ago, before there were any railways on Sodor, the Island was ruled by King Godred. He lived in a castle protected by knights and wore a golden crown. But one day the crown was stolen by thieves, never to be seen again. Now instead of knights in shining armour, railway engines rush around the Island . . .

King Godred's old castle at Ulfstead.

Meet the Steam Team!

Here are the famous Steam Team engines that work on The Fat Controller's Railway on Sodor. From grand Gordon to little Percy, the eight engines all have Really Useful jobs to do each day.

Henry   Edward   Percy   Thomas   James   Emily   Gordon

Toby

THOMAS
the Tank Engine

Thomas is the number 1 engine on the Island of Sodor. A cheeky tank engine, Thomas is friendly to everyone he meets. Thomas does lots of different jobs on the Island, including working on his very own branch line with his two carriages, Annie and Clarabel.

"I'm the number 1 blue engine!"

№1

AUGMENTED REALITY

Tap the "Play" button to start the AR, then help The Fat Controller to load Thomas by tapping on each crate in number order.

EDWARD
the Blue Engine

"A steady engine is a Really Useful Engine!"

Edward is a wise old engine and proudly wears the number 2 on his tender. He helps other engines when they run into trouble and even the Troublesome Trucks behave when Edward is pulling them! Edward's branch line runs from Brendam to Wellsworth.

Edward and Thomas are ready for another busy day

HENRY
the Green Engine

Long and fast, Henry sometimes pulls the Express when Gordon is busy. Henry was once a poorly engine and had to run on special coal. Now he has a new shape and feels much better, but he still worries more than most engines!

Henry and Thomas prepare for a special day on Sodor.

"Here comes Henry!"

№3

GORDON
the Big Express

"Look out! Express coming through!"

Big blue Gordon is the number 4 engine. Gordon is the fastest and most powerful of the Steam Team – but is he the fastest engine on Sodor? He certainly thinks he is and will challenge any engine to race him to prove it. Gordon doesn't like shunting trucks – his favourite job is pulling the Express.

Gordon and Spencer race to the finish!

JAMES
the Red Engine

Tender engine James has a fine scarlet coat and a shiny brass dome. He thinks he is a Really Splendid Engine and doesn't like doing any jobs that will make his red paint dirty. James can pull both passenger coaches and freight.

Nº5

"Mind my paintwork!"

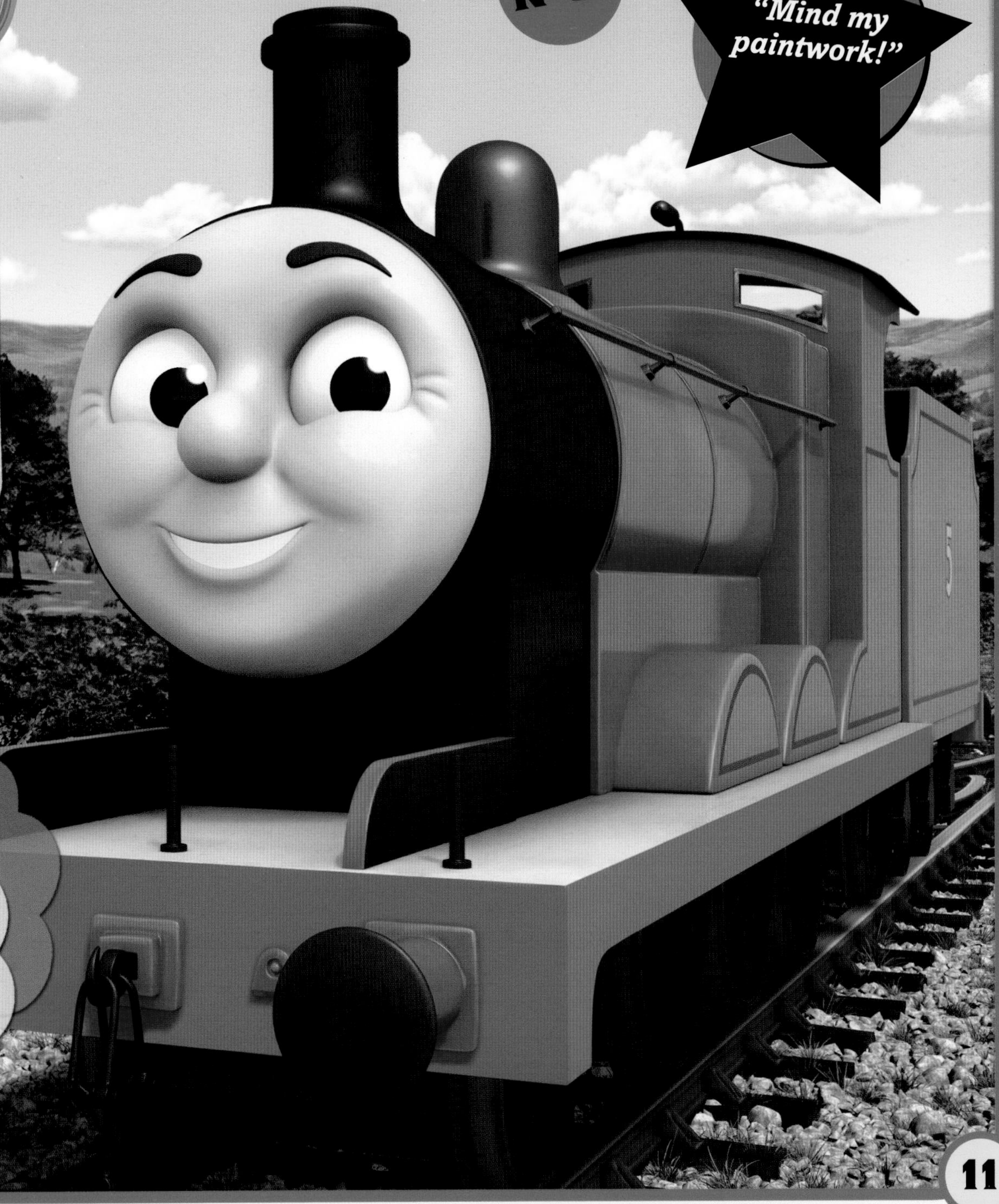

James gets very cross when he is dirty!

PERCY
the Small Engine

№6

"It's my job to deliver the mail!"

Percy is a little tank engine who is always ready for adventures with his best friend, Thomas. He keeps busy shunting trucks in the Yard and loves to pull the mail train. Percy may be small but he'll always puff his hardest to get the job done.

Percy and his friends are pulling a heavy freight train.

TOBY
the Tram Engine

Toby is a sturdy brown wooden tram engine. His number is 7. Toby loves to chuff up and down the Quarry line with his coach, Henrietta. Some of the engines think that he is old-fashioned, but Toby doesn't mind – he knows he is still a Really Useful Engine.

Toby and Thomas get along very well.

№7

"I'm a Really Useful Tram Engine!"

EMILY
the Stirling Single Engine

Emily is a beautiful emerald-green engine who has shiny brass fittings and two large driving wheels. She is a little bossy and likes to think that she knows best, but Emily is always ready to lend a wheel to any engine in trouble.

"I'm always ready to help a friend!"

Emily does all sorts of jobs on Sodor.

THE FAT CONTROLLER

"*Nothing is more important than my engines being Really Useful!*"

The Fat Controller is firm but fair with his engines.

Sir Topham Hatt, or The Fat Controller as he is known by his engines, is the director of the railway. It is his job to make sure that the engines run on time and do not cause delay! Sir Topham started out as an engineer and loves to travel by train whenever he can.

NEW FACES

In the exciting adventure, *King of the Railway*, some new engines arrive on the Island of Sodor. There is always room for new faces on The Fat Controller's Railway, but only Really Useful Engines are allowed to stay.

Poor **Millie** was stuck in a shed for years, but now she's ready to roll! Millie is a gauge engine who is painted a pretty shade of blue. The other engines are very pleased to meet her. Millie can carry plenty of passengers in her open-top coach.

Connor

Caitlin

Caitlin and **Connor**'s job is to bring passengers from the Mainland to visit Ulfstead Castle. Their streamlined shapes make them super-speedy – in fact, they are faster than both Gordon and Spencer!

The **Earl of Sodor** is an explorer who has returned home to the Island after many years of travelling. He wants to restore Ulfstead Castle, but he can't do it without the help of many Really Useful Engines.

Jack the friendly Front Loader is Thomas's old friend. He usually helps the Sodor Construction Crew, working on building jobs on the Island. But his help is needed elsewhere when an engine finds himself in trouble ...

The hero of *King of the Railway*, **Stephen** was one of the first steamies ever built. Turn the page to read more about him...

STEPHEN'S Story

Steam engine Stephen belongs to the Earl of Sodor. He is so old that he remembers when most railways didn't have engines and trains were pulled by horses! The Earl doesn't mind that Stephen is old – he has a very important job for Stephen to do when the Castle opens to visitors.

Percy, James and Thomas are excited to meet Stephen.

"I'm an antique!"

The Earl of Sodor shows off his old engine.

Cinders and Ashes!
Stephen's wheels haven't turned in years! With broken buffers, woodworm and rust, Stephen needs to be repaired from funnel to footplate before he's ready for the rails again!

LOOK AND SEE!
Stephen does not have an engine number on his side. Instead he has a nameplate with his nickname, 'the Rocket'.

New paintwork

Pistons on show

As good as new!

Polished brasswork

Fixed funnel

New boiler

Made almost entirely of wood

Mended buffers

Two large driving wheels

Thomas and Stephen soon become good friends.

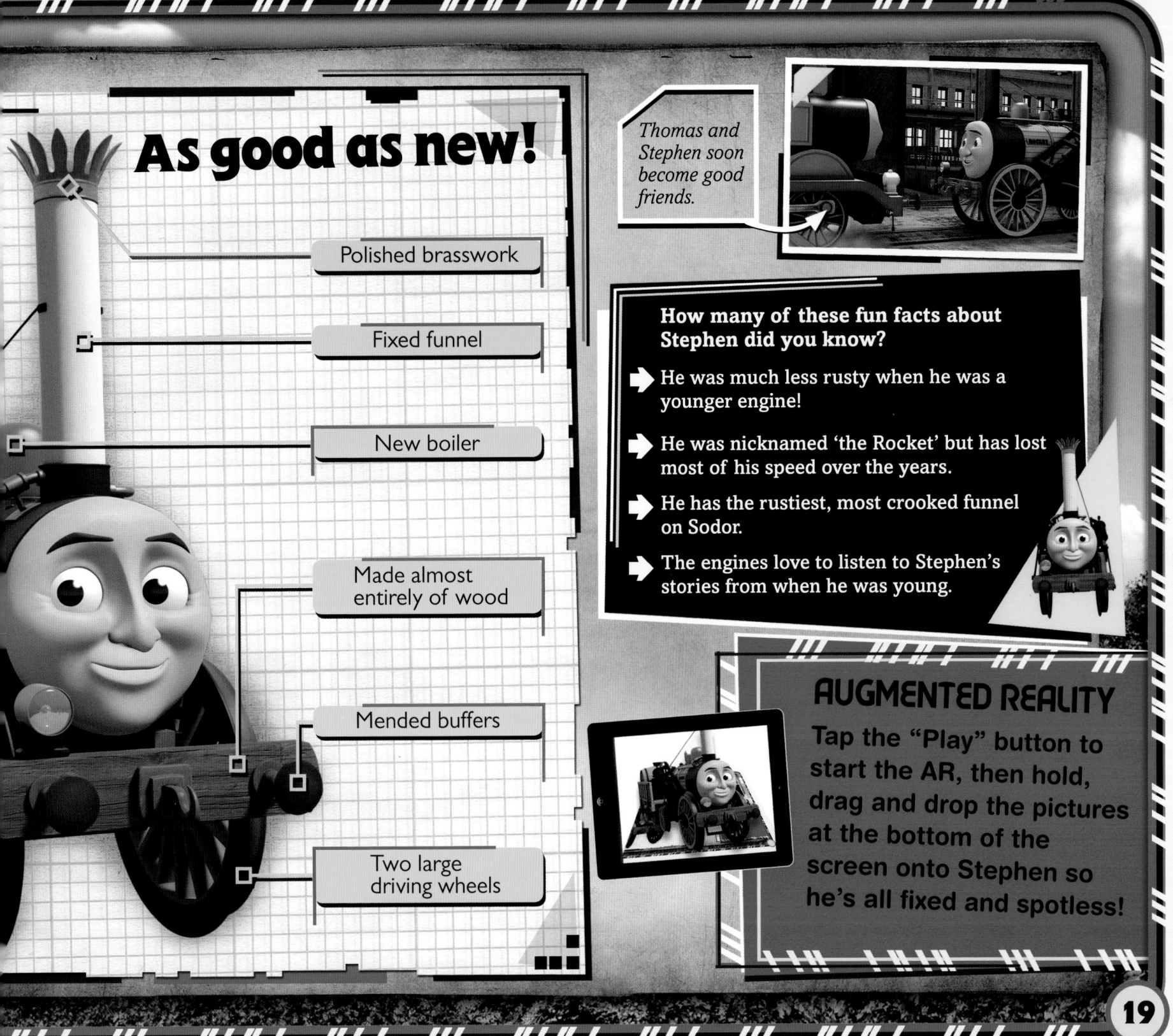

How many of these fun facts about Stephen did you know?

➤ He was much less rusty when he was a younger engine!

➤ He was nicknamed 'the Rocket' but has lost most of his speed over the years.

➤ He has the rustiest, most crooked funnel on Sodor.

➤ The engines love to listen to Stephen's stories from when he was young.

AUGMENTED REALITY

Tap the "Play" button to start the AR, then hold, drag and drop the pictures at the bottom of the screen onto Stephen so he's all fixed and spotless!

19

The STEAMWORKS

The Steamworks is one of the most important places on the Island. It's where the narrow gauge and standard gauge engines go for repairs. It's also where Victor and Kevin help Stephen get back on his wheels.

VICTOR

Victor is the manager of the Sodor Steamworks and has a very busy job. He looks after all the broken-down engines that come through his doors and can always find the right parts to fix his friends. He's a Really Useful Engine indeed!

KEVIN the Crane

Kevin is Victor's helper, but he isn't always that helpful! He's a friendly but clumsy crane who is ready and waiting to lend a helping hook. Kevin's accidents sometimes make Victor frown, but together they make a great team.

"I'll have you fixed up in no time!"

"Sorry, boss! It was a slip of the hook."

Fizzling Fireboxes!
When Victor sees Gordon, Emily, Henry, Edward and Toby puff into the Steamworks, he is worried – he thinks that all these engines need mending! But really they just want to see the new engine, Stephen.

FUN FACT
Although it is called the 'Sodor Steamworks', diesel engines have been repaired here too.

STEPHEN'S Quest

Stephen beams from bumper to buffer when he discovers he has a special job to do for the Earl! Like a brave knight of old, Stephen sets off on a quest to discover what his new job is . . .

Steamworks

Stephen asks at the Steamworks if anyone knows what his new job is, but neither Victor nor Kevin can tell him.

Victor doesn't know!

Kevin doesn't know!

'Brave Knight' Stephen sets off!

Diesel is rude to Stephen at Brendam Docks.

Brendam Docks

Next, Stephen heads to Brendam Docks but there isn't any work for him to do there. Diesel and Paxton are surprised to see such an old-fashioned engine.

Blue Mountain Quarry

Stephen puffs on to visit the Blue Mountain Quarry. The narrow gauge engines are hard at work, but Stephen isn't strong enough to help them pull heavy slate cars.

Luke, Rheneas and Skarloey at the Blue Mountain Quarry.

Poor Stephen decides that there isn't a job for him anywhere, as he thinks he is old, slow and weak.

Ulfstead Castle

Thomas later reveals that Stephen's real job is to be a guide at Ulfstead Castle and the new Estate. Stephen has never felt more proud!

Stephen finds his special job at Ulfstead Castle.

RAILWAY Rivalries

The engines on Sodor all want to be Really Useful workers. But sometimes when engines don't listen to instructions or think that they know best, they end up in a spot of bother! They soon learn that working together will get the job done quickly!

Speedy Steamies

Spencer thinks he is faster than Gordon because of his streamlined shape. Gordon says he's faster beause he pulls the big Express. Which engine do you think is faster?

Teamwork

The Fat Controller asks James, Thomas and Percy to pull a heavy goods train to the Earl's Estate. Each engine wants to pull the train on his own, but when they realize the train is so long, they are glad to work as a team!

Spencer speeds ahead of Gordon who is pulling a train of coaches.

Gordon is not pleased when he gets stuck behind Stephen on the track!

At the end of the King of the Railway story, The Fat Controller agrees that Gordon and Spencer can race each other to see who really is the fastest engine. Everyone comes to watch the big race!

Devious Diesels

Diesel engines, like dirty Diesel, are rude to Steamies and love to play tricks on them. Not all diesels are mean, though. Paxton is a much friendlier engine!

Streamlined Caitlin and Connor are speedier than all the engines on Sodor! They can whoosh past Gordon and Spencer in a blur.

Diesel

Paxton

AUGMENTED REALITY

Race Gordon and Spencer! Tap one of the "Play" buttons to choose your engine, then tap the racing button repeatedly to move your train along. Who will win the race?

ACCIDENTS
will happen!

Thomas and his friends know they must be careful when working on the Railway so that nobody gets hurt. But accidents happen now and again on Sodor, especially when engines are in a hurry. Here is a countdown of some of the crashes and close shaves from the *King of the Railway* story . . .

5 Many mishaps on Sodor are caused by the Troublesome Trucks! They think it's a joke to biff and bash the engines off the rails!

Bust My Buffers!
A dusty James huffs and puffs when he can't go straight to the Wash Down after the accident. His splendid paintwork looks a mess, but Thomas reminds him that Really Useful Engines must first finish their work.

2 When Percy moves too quickly, the wobbly scaffolding tower collapses in the Castle Courtyard, scattering stones and dust everywhere! Nobody is hurt, but Percy promises to pay more attention next time.

4 Kevin is so keen to please his boss, Victor, that he often tries to do things too quickly. There isn't a day that goes by without clumsy Kevin dropping or breaking something!

3 When Stephen tries to pull a line of heavy slate cars, he nearly comes off the track himself!

1 The most serious accident is when those Troublesome Trucks whoosh down the hill and crash into the mine. Thomas is relieved when they stop but he doesn't know that Stephen is trapped inside the mine!

Stephen tries to find a way out from the mine, but all the exits are blocked! Turn over to read more about the search for Stephen . . .

Calling all ENGINES!

When Thomas realises that Stephen could be in trouble, he calls on his friends to help him find the missing engine. All the engines, as well as the Sodor Search and Rescue Team, look for Stephen.

It's Thomas who finally tracks Stephen down, when he spots Stephen's broken funnel outside the blocked mineshaft.

Sodor Search and Rescue

IN THE AIR

"Duty calls!"

NAME: **Harold the Helicopter**

JOB: Harold hovers above the railways and roads, keeping a watchful eye on the engines on the ground. Harold will fly in any weather if a friend finds himself in trouble.

ON THE SEA

"Full speed ahead!"

NAME: **Captain the Lifeboat**

JOB: Captain is a wooden rescue boat and part of the Sodor Search and Rescue team. He always stays calm when out on emergency patrols on the seas around Sodor.

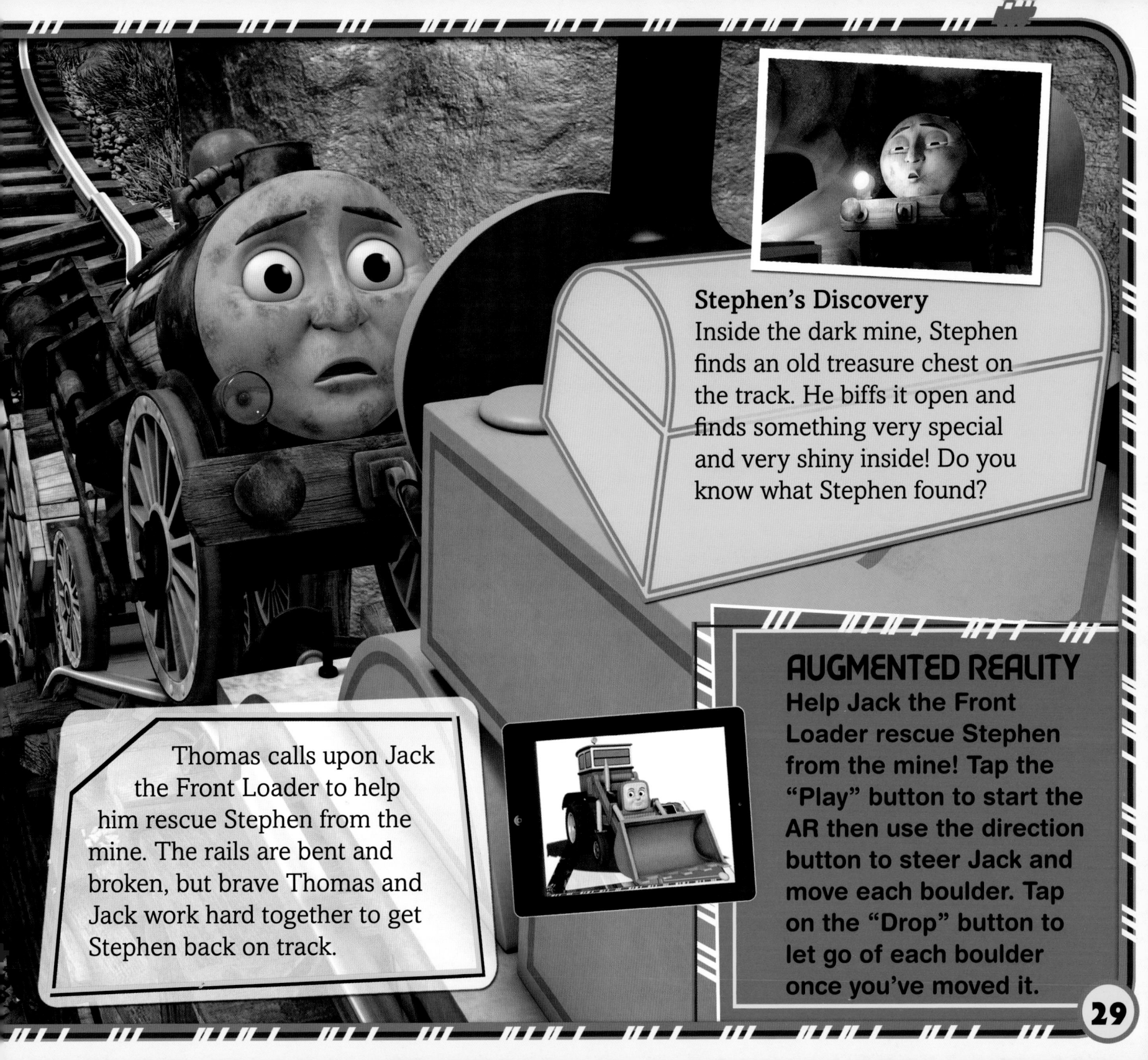

Stephen's Discovery

Inside the dark mine, Stephen finds an old treasure chest on the track. He biffs it open and finds something very special and very shiny inside! Do you know what Stephen found?

AUGMENTED REALITY

Help Jack the Front Loader rescue Stephen from the mine! Tap the "Play" button to start the AR then use the direction button to steer Jack and move each boulder. Tap on the "Drop" button to let go of each boulder once you've moved it.

Thomas calls upon Jack the Front Loader to help him rescue Stephen from the mine. The rails are bent and broken, but brave Thomas and Jack work hard together to get Stephen back on track.

...e Earl brings a suit of armour to ...ess up in so he looks like a knight ...

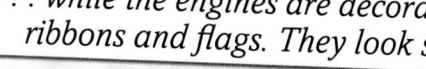

... while the engines are decorated with ribbons and flags. They look smart!

Golden Crown

In the old treasure chest, Stephen finds a golden crown that belonged to King Godred. The crown had been missing for a long time after thieves stole it many years ago. The Earl of Sodor is very happy when Stephen finds the crown in the mine. Now everyone can see the precious treasure!

USEFUL JOBS

✔ **Connor and Caitlin**
Bring visitors from the Mainland

✔ **Stephen**
Show visitors around the Castle

✔ **Millie**
Bring the Earl of Sodor to the Castle

✔ **Thomas**
Bring special guests to the Castle

✔ **Gordon, James, Percy and Jack**
Join in the celebrations!

Famous Funnel

Stephen's new funnel is painted to look like a crown especially for the celebrations! Now Stephen looks like Railway Royalty. Some even call him 'The King of the Railway'!

Can you find
these pictures
in the book?